A LITTLE BOOK FOR

CHRISTMAS

Published in 2022 by OH!
An Imprint of Welbeck Non-Fiction Limited,
part of Welbeck Publishing Group.
Based in London and Sydney.
www.welbeckpublishing.com

Compilation text © Welbeck Non-Fiction Limited 2022
Design © Welbeck Non-Fiction Limited 2022

ISBN 978-1-80069-236-7

Compiled and written by: Marcus Leaver
Editorial: Stella Caldwell
Design: Stephen Cary
Project manager: Russell Porter
Production: Jess Brisley

A CIP catalogue record for this book is available from the British Library

Printed in China

10 9 8 7 6 5 4 3 2 1

Illustrations: Shutterstock

A LITTLE BOOK FOR
CHRISTMAS

A COLLECTION OF GLAD
TIDINGS AND FESTIVE CHEER

CONTENTS

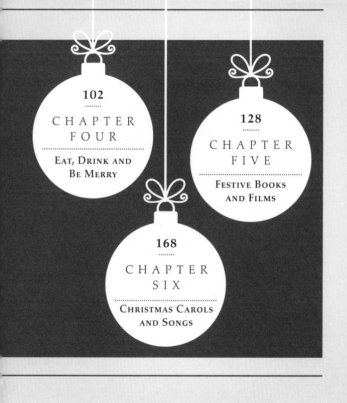

Dear Christmas Lover,

It was a delight to collate the tidbits of Christmas history and traditions, and wonderful festive quotes, to put into this small but perfectly formed little book about Christmas and our love of this time of year. I have enjoyed every minute spent choosing what to include.

The book is just my take on the subject and the delight Christmas gives me and my family. As with any miscellany, you will be delighted to come across familiar items and much-loved quotes and sayings, and perhaps disappointed to see that others have been left out. Hopefully, however, the Yuletide lover will find something contained within these pages to delight, inform or entertain them – and to bring a warm glow of festive cheer.

HAPPY READING.

Marcus E. Leaver
London

CHAPTER ONE

The Origins of Christmas

If you want to be the most knowledgeable person at the Christmas table, look no further! Learn the meaning of the name Bethlehem, find out who set 25 December as Jesus' birthday and discover how Good King Wenceslas wasn't a king at all…

> 66
> # What is Christmas? It is tenderness for the past, courage for the present, hope for the future.
> 99

Agnes M. Pahro

66

Christmas is a
season not only
of rejoicing but of
reflection.

99

Winston Churchill

The nativity of Jesus is only mentioned in two out of the New Testament's 27 books: Matthew and Luke.

In Hebrew, the name Bethlehem means "house of bread".

In Arabic, it means "house of meat".

For centuries, astronomers have tried to find a scientific explanation for the Star of Bethlehem.

Theories have included a supernova, a comet, a solar flare and an alignment of planets, but there is no real evidence that any of these things occurred at the time of Jesus' birth.

How many wise men were there? The Bible doesn't actually tell us! Western tradition states there were three, while Eastern orthodoxy claims there were 12.

In 2004, the Church of
England Synod agreed
that the term "Magi", as
used in the Bible, was the
name used for officials at
the Persian court.

This means that Jesus'
visiting Magi were not
necessarily wise –
or even men.

The three Magi are commonly known as Melchior, Caspar and Balthazar. In Western tradition, Melchior was a king of Persia, Caspar a king of India and Balthazar a king of Arabia or Ethiopia.

Although we can't be sure
of the number of wise men, we
do know there were
three gifts.

GOLD was a symbol of
kingship and glory and also
of Jesus' divinity.

FRANKINCENSE is made
from the aromatic resin of the
Boswellia tree.
It was given as a sign of Jesus'
purity.

MYRRH is an aromatic resin,
used as a perfume, incense
and medicine.
It was given as a symbol
of mortality.

Christmas is predated by two major pagan festivals. The Roman festival of

SATURNALIA

honoured the god Saturn, while the Norse festival of

YULE

was a 12-day feast celebrated around the winter solstice.

In 350 CE, Pope Julius I decreed 25 December as Christmas Day.

It may have been an attempt to absorb the traditions of the Roman Saturnalia festival.

On Christmas Day in 597 CE, St Augustine of Canterbury reportedly baptized 10,000 Englishmen as Christians.

The word Christmas comes from the Anglo-Saxon word

CRISTES MAESSE

meaning "Christ's Mass". It was first seen in a book dating from 1038 CE.

Saint Francis of Assisi staged the first live nativity scene, in 1223. The first known nativity figurines were displayed in Rome's Church of Santa Maria Maggiore, in the late 13th century.

In 1647, when England was under Puritan rule, Parliament passed an act banning the celebration of Christmas.

King Charles II, known as the "Merry Monarch", restored it in 1660.

For around four centuries, Christmas was effectively banned in Scotland.

After the Reformation in 1560, the Presbyterians saw Christmas as a Catholic festival and it was downgraded to a normal working day. It didn't become a public holiday until 1958!

"Good" King Wenceslas was a real person, though he wasn't a king. Born around 907 CE, he was a duke of Bohemia.

Credited with bringing Christianity to his people, he became the patron saint of the Czech Republic.

We are better
throughout the year
for having, in spirit,
become a child again
at Christmastime.

Laura Ingalls Wilder

66

When we recall
Christmas past, we usually
find that the simplest
things – not the great
occasions – give off the
greatest glow of happiness.

99

Bob Hope

CHAPTER TWO

Deck The Halls

In the 1840s, an engraving showing Queen Victoria and Prince Albert celebrating Christmas around a tree established a new festive craze. As the following pages show, the German tradition of the Christmas tree is just one of many fascinating customs from around the world.

"

Promise you will be

Nobody else's little
Christmas tree

I'll make you sparkle, just
you wait and see

My little Christmas tree...

"

From "The Little Christmas Tree", Nat King Cole

66

I've learned that you can
tell a lot about a person by
the way he handles these
three things:
a rainy day, lost luggage
and tangled
Christmas tree lights.

99

Maya Angelou

The Christmas wreath has its roots in the pagan festival of Saturnalia.

The Romans decorated their houses and buildings with wreaths made from holly, fir and ivy.

Britain's first Christmas tree was displayed by Queen Charlotte, the German wife of George III, in 1800.

However, it was the German-born husband of Queen Victoria, Prince Albert, who popularized the tradition in the 1840s.

Before Christmas trees were adorned with fairy lights, it was customary to use lighted candles.

As beeswax candles were expensive, many people used tallow candles made from animal fat. This led to a distinct aroma and a very smoky house.

In 1847, Hans Greiner of Lauscha, Germany produced the first glass tree ornaments, in the shape of fruit and nuts.

By the 1880s, they had become all the rage in the UK and the US.

The famous Christmas tree displayed in London's Trafalgar Square is an annual gift from the people of Oslo, Norway, in thanks for the UK's help during the Second World War.

At around 21 m (70 ft) tall, it is decorated in typical Norwegian fashion with vertical strings of lights.

America's national Christmas tree is located in King's Canyon, California.

A living giant sequoia, it is more than 90 m (300 ft) tall and is known as the General Grant tree.

The custom of sending

CHRISTMAS CARDS

was started by
Sir Henry Cole in 1843.

With the help of an artist
friend, John Horsley, he
designed a card featuring three
panels – the outer panels showed
people caring for the poor,
while the centre panel showed
a wealthy family enjoying
Christmas dinner.

Henry Cole produced 2,050 Christmas cards, selling them for a shilling each.

However, the design, showing people drinking wine, proved controversial, as some believed it promoted drunkenness!

In the early 19th century, German Protestants began marking the days of Advent by lighting a candle or making a mark on a wall each day.

The first known Advent calendar, made of wood, appeared in 1851.

The first printed
Advent calendar appeared
around 1902.

In 1958, the first
Advent calendar with
chocolate was produced
in the US.

The UK's official definition of a "White Christmas" is "one snowflake to be observed falling in the 24 hours of 25 December somewhere in the UK".

That's happened 38 times since 1970. However, a proper blanket of snow has only been recorded four times since 1960.

In India,
banana and mango
trees are decorated at
Christmas time.

The turkey has its origins in Mexico.

Wild turkeys were first domesticated there around 2,000 years ago.

A female domesticated turkey is called a hen and its chick is known as a poult.

In the US, the male is called a tom, while in the UK it's called a stag.

Queen Victoria's
Christmas Day menu for 1894
included calf's head consommé,
puréed pheasant meat,
roast beef and roast turkey,
woodcock pie, mince pies, plum
pudding and jellied orange-
flavoured custards.

Also on the menu were wild
boar's head (a gift from
the Emperor of Germany)
and terrine de foie gras (a
gift from the Grand Duke of
Mecklenburg-Schwerin).

66

At dinner there were all the Christmas dishes, of which we generally had to eat a little: first the cold baron of beef which stood on the large sideboard all decked out – brawn – game pies from Ireland and others – stuffed turkey – wild boar's head – which Albert was so fond of – mince pies etc etc.

99

Extract from Queen Victoria's diary

Poinsettia, with its vibrant red leaves, comes from Mexico, where it is known as the "Flower of the Holy Night".

It is named after the first American ambassador to Mexico, Dr Joel Roberts Poinsett, after he brought the plant back to the US in 1829.

The town of
ENCINITAS
in California is now
recognized as the
Poinsettia capital of
the world because of
the profusion of
plants there.

The word "Yule" comes from the Old English word *geol*, which shares a history with the equivalent word from Old Norse, *jól*.

The custom of burning the Yule log was a Nordic tradition that started well before medieval times.

As the winter solstice approached, families ventured out to select the largest log they could find. Placed on the fire, the log was kept burning through the 12 days of Christmas.

In Sweden, straw Yule goats are placed around homes during the festive season.

In the town of Gävle, a giant straw goat is erected each year. It is a tradition for pranksters to burn or destroy the goat before celebrations even begin!

Today the Yule log
has become an edible
chocolate dessert – and
for chocolate lovers,
the focus of Christmas
eating.

What has the Belgian capital got to do with sprouts?

There are records of Brussels sprouts in the area of Brussels as far back as the 13th century, though it's not certain if that's where they were first cultivated.

You may not like them –
but Brussels sprouts are good
for you!

Like cabbages, they are
members of the cruciferous
family of vegetables, which
are a fine source of the
antioxidant vitamins A and
C, potassium and iron.

The delicious

MINCE PIE,

filled with rich spiced fruit, is
enjoyed throughout much of
the English-speaking world.

The reason the filling is
called mincemeat is because
that's exactly what it used to be.
In medieval times,
large "Christmas pyes" were
filled with mutton, beef, pork,
rabbit or game.

66

The sermon done, a good anthem followed, with vialls, and then the King came down to receive the Sacrament … I walked home again with great pleasure, and there dined by my wife's bed-side with great content, having a mess of brave plum-porridge and a roasted pullet for dinner, and I sent for a mince-pie abroad…

99

From the diary of Samuel Pepys, Christmas Day, 1662

"

At Christmas play and
make good cheer

For Christmas comes
but once a year.

"

Thomas Tusser

Fish is enjoyed on Christmas Eve throughout Europe.

In Poland, the fish of choice is carp, while in Portugal and Croatia it is salt cod.

The Hungarians eat "Fishermen's Stew", made from carp, catfish and perch.

In Sweden, there's an abundance of herring at the table, served either pickled or in a salad.

Mulled wine was first made by the Romans, who added honey, spices and dates to boiled red wine.

By the 13th century, "spiced wine" had become popular in England – by all accounts, it was a favourite drink of Henry III.

MULLED WINE

Around the World

Germany – **Glühwein**

Scandinavia – **Glögg**

Canada – **Caribou**

The Netherlands – **Bischopswijn**

France – **Vin Chaud**

Slovenia – **Kuhano Vino**

Stealing a kiss under the mistletoe is a tradition that goes back to our pre-Christian past.

The Celtic people believed mistletoe had healing properties.

For the Romans, it was a symbol of peace used in the Saturnalia celebrations.

"

Mistletoe from
The Christmas oak,
Keep my house
From lightning stroke.

Guard from thunder
My roof-tree
And any evil
That there be.

"

From "Mistletoe" by Charles Causley

Italians around the world celebrate Christmas Eve with the Feast of the Seven Fishes, or the *cenone* in Italian. Why the number seven was chosen is a matter of dispute.

Some suggest it represents the Seven Sacraments of the Catholic Church. Others believe it stands for the seven deadly sins, or perhaps the seven wonders of the world.

66

Christmas waves a magic wand over the world, and behold, everything is softer and more beautiful.

99

Norman Vincent Peale

CHAPTER THREE

Santa Claus

Whether you call him Santa, Father Christmas or Papa Noel, the red-suited, bearded man who creeps into our homes each year is one of the most recognizable figures in modern culture. Discover the fascinating history behind "Jolly Old St Nick" and explore present-giving traditions around the world.

"

One of the most glorious messes in the world is the mess created in the living room on Christmas Day. Don't clean it up too quickly.

"

Andy Rooney

"

I stopped believing
in Santa Claus when
I was six. Mother
took me to see him
in a department store
and he asked for my
autograph.

"

Shirley Temple

Behind the jolly, red-suited figure of Santa Claus lies a real person: St Nicholas of Myra (modern-day Demre, in Turkey).

The day of his death – 6 December – is known as St Nicholas Day, when he is celebrated as the patron saint of children and the bringer of gifts.

In Eastern Christian countries, the feast is celebrated on 19 December, according to the old Church calendar.

The tradition of hanging stockings by the fire or the foot of the bed dates back to the time of St Nicholas.

One legend tells how he secretly helped a poor father with his daughters' dowries by dropping gold coins down the chimney.

Children began hanging up stockings, or putting out their shoes, in the hope of benefiting from his generosity.

Have you ever wondered why tangerines are given in Christmas stockings?

The legend dates back to French nuns in the 12th century, who left socks full of fruit and nuts at the houses of the poor.

SANTA CLAUS

Around the World

The UK – **Father Christmas**

The Netherlands – **Sinterklaas**

Finland – **Joulupukki**
("Christmas Goat")

China – **Sheng dan lao ren**
("Christmas Old Man")

France – **Père Noël**

Denmark – **Julemanden**
("The Yule Man")

Greece – **Ayios Vassileios**

Brazil – **Papai Noel**

"

Everything was now ready for tomorrow. There was nothing to do except go to bed, curl up in our blankets and wait, each with his long stocking hanging on the bedpost, empty…

Would there be a flash of red in the window, a snow-glint of beard and ermine, a whisper of sleigh bells on our rooftops as Father Christmas made his benevolent entrance?

"

Laurie Lee, Village Christmas

66

You better watch out

You better not cry

You better not pout

I'm telling you why

Santa Claus is comin' to town!

99

From "Santa Claus is comin' to town",
first recorded in 1934

In many parts of Germany, the Christkind, or Christkindl, is the traditional gift bringer. She is depicted as a young girl with Christ-like qualities.

Children write a letter to her asking for presents, and glue sugar to the envelope to make it sparkle.

As a result of Germans emigrating to the US, the Christkindl became *Kris Kringle* in that part of the world.

It has become a synonym for the gift exchange tradition also known as "Secret Santa".

Santa Claus has featured in Coca-Cola ads since the 1920s. Prior to that, he was often depicted as tall and gaunt, a far cry from the jolly, plump figure we recognize today.

Coca-Cola's advertising helped to shape the modern version of Santa as a warm, cheerful figure – although it is a myth that the drinks company was responsible for his red coat.

Santa Claus' official post office can be found just north of Rovaniemi, the capital of Lapland, in northern Finland.

He receives around 600,000 letters each year.

"

We celebrated Christmas.
Not religiously, but we
did the tree and the
lights. Hannukah always
seemed not quite as
thrilling – Sorry to my
Jewish brothers and
sisters!

But when you're a kid, Santa and all that, you know, that really trumps the menorah. So we did Christmas.

99

Matthew Broderick

In Spain and Latin America, it is the Three Kings who bring presents.

Children leave out their shoes to receive gifts on 6 January.

On the night of 5 January,
excited Italian children
hang up their stockings in
anticipation of a late-night
visit from a kindly old witch
called La Befana.

She brings them gifts
and sweets if they have
been good, and coal if
they haven't.

An old Russian folktale tells of how Baboushka, which means "grandmother", travelled far and wide looking for the newborn king.

She didn't find him, but as she searched, she visited the homes of children and left presents for them while they slept in their beds.

In Scandinavia, gift-giving is the job of a tribe of gnomes called **Nisse**.

In return, they expect to receive a large bowl of porridge and perhaps a mug of beer.

The iconic poem
"Twas the Night Before Christmas"
was penned by American Episcopalian Minister Clement Clarke Moore in 1822.

Or was it?

Some believe it was actually the work of Henry Livingston Jr, a veteran of the American Revolution – though there is no physical evidence for this claim.

"Twas the night before Christmas,
when all through the house

Not a creature was stirring, not even
a mouse;

The stockings were hung by the
chimney with care,

In hopes that St Nicholas soon
would be there;

The children were nestled all snug in
their beds;

While visions of sugar-plums danced
in their heads…"

*Clement Clarke Moore,
"The Night Before Christmas", 1822*

Eight reindeer are featured in "Twas the Night Before Christmas", though none of them are called Rudolph!

He didn't appear until 1939, as a character in a poem written by copywriter Robert L. May. He was commissioned to write a Christmas story in a bid to draw more shoppers to Montgomery Ward Store in Chicago.

Robert May named the underdog reindeer in his story Rudolph at the suggestion of his four-year-old daughter.

She preferred that name over Rollo or Reginald.

'Ha ha! Look at Rudolph!
His nose is a sight!

It's red as a beet! Twice as
big! Twice as bright!'

*From the original poem "Rudolph, the Red-Nosed
Reindeer" by Robert L. May*

**"Rudolph
the Red-Nosed
Reindeer"**
became a song
in 1949, composed by
Johnny Marks
and first recorded by
Gene Autry.

Reindeer are the only deer that can be domesticated.

It is believed domestication first took place between 3,000 and 1,000 years ago, in eastern Russia.

Reindeer are unable to walk and pee at the same time, and need to urinate roughly every 6 miles (9.5 km). In Finnish, this distance is known as

PORONKUSEMA

or "reindeer's piss", and was once used as a description of distance.

66

No matter what, I always make it home for Christmas. I love to go to my Tennessee mountain home and invite all of my nieces and nephews and their spouses and kids

and do what we all
like to do – eat, laugh,
trade presents and
just enjoy each other...
and sometimes
I even dress up like
Santa Claus!

Dolly Parton

Gift-giving at Christmas
has both Christian and pagan
origins.

In Christian tradition, it
mimics the three gifts the
Magi, or wise men, brought
the baby Jesus. But the custom
also has roots in the ancient
Roman festival of Saturnalia,
when people gave offerings
to the gods.

In 1867, Macy's department store in New York City remained open until midnight on Christmas Eve for the first time, thereby staking claim to the tradition of last-minute Christmas shopping.

I don't think Christmas
is necessarily about
things. It's about being
good to one another.

Carrie Fisher

100

"

My mom and dad always tried to make Christmas special for us. We were poor, but it's funny because we had no idea.

"

Johnny Mathis

CHAPTER FOUR

Eat, Drink and Be Merry

Christmas just wouldn't be Christmas without delicious food and drink. But have you ever wondered what people from other countries eat on the big day? From Cuban eggnog to Bibingka from the Philippines, the following selection of festive treats will give you a taste of Christmas around the world.

EGGNOG

United States and Canada

This drink, made with eggs, sugar, milk, cream and vanilla extract – and traditionally spiked with brandy – may be American, but it has its roots in England.

It is believed to have originated with medieval monks who drank "posset" – a warm ale punch made with eggs and figs.

"

Now Christmas comes, 'tis fit that we

should feast and sing, and merry be:

Keep open house, let fiddlers play.

A fig for cold, sing care away;

And may they who thereat repine,

On brown bread and on small beer dine.

"

From the 1766 Virginia Almanack

COUGNOU

Belgium

Tasting a bit like the sweet
French brioche, this
Christmas bread takes the form
of the swaddled infant Jesus.

66

All families had their special Christmas food. Ours was called Dutch Bread, made from a dough halfway between bread and cake, stuffed with citron and every sort of nut from the farm – hazel, black walnut, hickory, butternut.

99

Paul Engle

PAN DE PASCUA

Chile

Despite its name, this is a cake rather than a bread.

The sponge is flavoured with bits of candied fruits, raisins, walnuts and almonds.

CREMA DE VIE

Cuba

This Cuban eggnog, made
with condensed milk, rum,
lemon rind and spices,
is served as a festive treat.

It is often given as a present
in a fancy bottle.

My grandmother did all the cooking at Christmas. We ate fattened chicken. We would feed it even more so it would be big and fat.

Alain Ducasse

THIRTEEN DESSERTS

Provence, France

This age-old Provençal tradition states that 13 desserts must be served after the main Christmas meal. Representing Jesus and the 12 apostles, the desserts, ranging from dried figs to nougat, are traditionally set out on Christmas Eve and remain on the table until 27 December.

CHRISTSTOLLEN

Germany

The Christmas stollen is a fruit cake with bits of candied fruits, raisins, walnuts and almonds, and spices such as cardamom and cinnamon.

It is sprinkled with icing sugar and often contains a core of marzipan.

GINGERBREAD HOUSE

Germany

The Christmas tradition of the gingerbread house (*lebkuchenhaus*), decorated with icing and sweets, began in the early 1800s.

It was popularized by the Hansel and Gretel fairytale, which described two children stumbling across a house made entirely of treats.

MÖNDLUGRAUTUR

Iceland

This simple rice pudding
has an almond hidden
inside – whoever finds it gets
a special treat!

ALLAHABADI CAKE

India

Borrowing its name from the north Indian city of Allahabad, this traditional fruit cake is made with pure ghee and spices such as nutmeg, cinnamon, fennel, mace and ginger.

CHRISTMAS PUDDING

United Kingdom

Christmas dinner in the UK would not be complete without a Christmas pudding, traditionally served with brandy sauce or brandy butter. Also known as plum or "figgy" pudding, it began life as a medieval "pottage", a kind of broth containing wine, dried fruit and spices.

"

In half a minute Mrs Cratchit
entered – flushed, but smiling
proudly – with the pudding, like a
speckled cannon ball, so
hard and firm, blazing in half of
half-a-quartern of ignited brandy,
and bedight with Christmas holly
stuck into the top.
Oh, a wonderful pudding!

"

Charles Dickens, A Christmas Carol

BIBINGKA
The Philippines

During the Christmas season, Filipinos like to eat this spongy rice cake with another type of rice cake called *puto bumbong*. It can be garnished with salted egg and white cheese made from carabao milk, slathered with butter and topped with grated coconut.

TRONCO DE NATAL

Portugal

No Portuguese Christmas is complete without this version of the chocolate Yule log. A swiss-roll sponge cake is covered in rich chocolate ganache, and marked to look like a log.

COZONAC
Romania

This simple, sweetened yeast bread is traditionally made at Christmas and Easter.

It tastes a little like the Italian panettone, though it is denser and usually has a filling, such as walnuts or dried fruit, inside.

ČESNICA

Serbia

An indispensable part of
Serbian festivities, this round
loaf is baked with a silver
coin inside. Whoever finds
the coin should have good
health and fortune!

SPANISH KINGS' CAKE

Spain

The *roscón de reyes* is a crown-shaped cake hiding a baby Jesus figurine, trinket, dried bean or sweet inside. Tradition says that whoever finds the hidden treat pays for the cake!

JULBORD

Sweden

A classic Swedish Christmas
buffet, or *julbord*, includes a great
many dishes, such as *knäckebröd*
(crispbread), pickled herring,
gravlax (cured salmon), crayfish,
cold slices of ham, *köttbullar*
(meatballs), beetroot salad and
janssons frestelse, a baked casserole
made with creamy potatoes.

PANETTONE

Italy

At Christmas, Italian bakeries display beautifully wrapped and decorated panettone.

This cake-like bread, stuffed with raisins and candied orange and lemon peel, originated in Milan in the 15th century.

66

Panettone,
più torrone,
più capitone,
più cenone,
uguale a indigestione.

99

*This translates as "Panettone, and nougat, and a
large eel, and a Christmas dinner, means you'll
have indigestion"!*

BLACK CAKE

Jamaica

This decadent, rum-soaked
fruit cake is eaten throughout
the Caribbean during the
festive season.

KAPUSTNICA

Czech Republic and Slovakia

This cabbage soup, traditionally
served as the first course
on Christmas Eve, almost
always contains mushrooms
and perhaps smoked meat or
sausage.

CHAPTER FIVE

Festive Books and Films

What could be better than grabbing a hot chocolate and settling down to a seasonal book or film? Find out when Father Christmas first appeared in print, learn why we love to tell spooky tales on Christmas Eve, and discover which holiday movies we love to watch again and again!

Charles Dickens' earliest piece of festive writing was a short sketch, *A Christmas Dinner*, published in 1835.

Describing a delightful family gathering, it provides a wonderful insight into how Christmas Day was celebrated at the time.

66

Uncle George tells stories, and carves poultry, and takes wine, and jokes with the children at the side-table … and exhilarates everybody with his good humour and hospitality; and when, at last, a stout servant staggers in with a gigantic pudding, with a sprig of holly in the top, there is such a laughing, and shouting, and clapping of little chubby hands … Then the dessert! – and the wine! – and the fun!

99

Charles Dickens, A Christmas Dinner, *1835*

Father Christmas made his first literary appearance in a festive piece of writing by Shakespeare's contemporary Ben Jonson.

Christmas, His Masque presents the character of "Old Christmas" with a long thin beard and wearing a doublet and hose and a "high-crowned hat". It was performed for the royal court in 1616.

66

Fine old Christmas, with the snowy hair and ruddy face, had done his duty that year in the noblest fashion, and had set off his rich gifts of warmth and colour with all the heightening contrast of frost and snow.

99

George Eliot, The Mill on the Floss, *1860*

Hans Christian Andersen's poignant winter tale *The Little Match Girl* has become a Christmas classic. It tells of a poor girl lighting matches to warm herself on New Year's Eve.

In the flame, she sees visions of a Christmas tree and a delicious feast. Andersen believed the devastating ending to be a happy one, as the girl finds herself in heaven.

Tolkien's *Letters from Father Christmas*, first published in 1976, is a series of letters written to the author's children between 1920 and 1942.

They document what Father Christmas has been up to at the North Pole and describe characters such as his polar-bear assistant, and goblins who break into his cellars to steal presents.

FESTIVE FICTION

*Eight books to get you in the mood
for Christmas*

The Nutcracker – E.T.A. Hoffmann

The Twelve Terrors of Christmas
– John Updike and Edward Gorey

The Snow Child – Eowyn Ivey

Holidays on Ice – David Sedaris

Christmas Days – Jeanette
Winterson

Little Women – Louisa May Alcott

Village Christmas – Laurie Lee

Christmas at Cold Comfort Farm
– Stella Gibbons

"

Christmas always rustled.
It rustled every time,
mysteriously, with silver and
gold paper, tissue paper and a
rich abundance of shiny paper,
decorating and hiding
everything and giving a feeling
of reckless extravagance.

"

*Moomin creator Tove Jansson, in her
childhood memoir* Sculptor's Daughter, *1968*

"

I have received and read all the letters which you and your little sister have written me … I can read your and your baby sister's jagged and fantastic marks without any trouble at all … I went down your chimney at midnight when you were asleep and delivered them all myself…

"

Mark Twain, A Letter from Santa Claus, *sent to his three-year old daughter, Susie, 1875*

Jean-Paul Sartre's first ever play was a nativity play called *Baronia, or The Son of Thunder*. It was performed on Christmas Eve in 1940 by prisoners at the German prisoner-of-war camp where Sartre was himself imprisoned during the Second World War.

Sartre later said that he saw the play as a way of creating unity amongst his fellow prisoners.

Charles Dickens wrote
A Christmas Carol in just
six weeks. Published on
19 December 1843, it
had already sold out by
Christmas Eve.

Rapturously received, it has
remained Dickens' most
widely enjoyed work, with
countless further reprints
and adaptations.

66

'If I could work my will,' said Scrooge indignantly, 'every idiot who goes about with "Merry Christmas" on his lips, should be boiled with his own pudding, and buried with a stake of holly through his heart. He should!'

99

Charles Dickens, A Christmas Carol, *1843*

The tradition of telling spooky stories around Christmas is connected to the winter solstice, a time when light is scarce and the veil between the worlds of the living and the dead seems thin.

In Victorian times, gathering around the fire to tell ghost stories became a beloved tradition.

SEASON'S SCREAMINGS!

Five ghostly tales for Christmas Eve

The Old Nurse's Story – Elizabeth Gaskell

The Turn of the Screw – Henry James

The Kit-Bag – Algernon Blackwood

Oh, Whistle and I'll Come to You, My Lad – M.R. James

Christmas Present – Ramsey Campbell

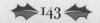

"

Then the Grinch thought of something he hadn't before!

What if Christmas, he thought, doesn't come from a store.

What if Christmas … perhaps … means a little bit more!

"

Dr Seuss, How the Grinch Stole Christmas, *1957*

It's a common misconception that the much-loved Grinch first appeared in Dr Seuss's *How the Grinch Stole Christmas* in 1957.

However, he actually made his debut two years earlier in the author's poem "The Hoobub and the Grinch".

Michael Bond claimed that his creation Paddington Bear came about after a last-minute purchase on Christmas Eve, in 1956.

He saw a solitary teddy bear on a London shop shelf, and, feeling sorry that nobody wanted the poor toy, decided to buy it himself. He named the bear Paddington after nearby Paddington Station – and the rest is history.

66

'One can never have
enough socks,' said
Dumbledore. 'Another
Christmas has come and
gone and I didn't get a
single pair. People will
insist on giving me books.'

99

J.K. Rowling, Harry Potter and the
Philosopher's Stone, *1997*

66

Always winter and never Christmas; think of that!

99

C.S. Lewis, The Lion, the Witch and the Wardrobe, *1950*

$\mathcal{S}$anta first appeared on film in a silent British short, *Santa Claus*, in 1898.

It was directed by George Albert Smith, who pioneered the practice of film editing and the usage of close-ups.

Early Christmas films used white-painted cornflakes to emulate snow.

This presented a problem for *It's a Wonderful Life* in 1946, as director Frank Capra wanted to record the sound live during the snow scenes, and the cornflakes crunching underfoot made this impossible!

A new kind of snow, made from foamite, sugar, soap flakes and water, was produced for filming.

Although it's now celebrated as a true Christmas classic, things weren't always wonderful for *It's a Wonderful Life*.

The movie bombed on its release in 1946, and leading man James Stewart, feared it might prove fatal to his career.

It was not until the 1960s that the film began to enjoy a renaissance.

66

Strange, isn't it?
Each man's life touches
so many other lives.
When he isn't around,
he leaves an awful hole,
doesn't he?

99

Clarence, to George, It's a Wonderful Life, *1946*

Festive favourite *Home Alone* references another Christmas movie.

The family is shown watching *It's a Wonderful Life* in their hotel room in France.

The Nightmare Before Christmas was shot at 24 frames per second.

This means that for each second of the movie, the characters had to be posed 24 times.

To shoot each minute of the film took an entire week to complete.

While playing the lead role in
How the Grinch Stole Christmas,
Jim Carrey had to withstand
hours of make-up work that
involved being covered head to
foot in green fur and wearing
enlarged contact lenses.

The process was so traumatic
that Carrey worked with a CIA
specialist who trained agents how
to survive torture.

"

No one should be alone
on Christmas.

"

How the Grinch Stole Christmas, *2000*

The Disney hit
Frozen, based on the story
The Snow Queen by
Hans Christian Andersen,
was first suggested as a
possible film in 1939.

It took 70 years before it
was produced and released.

Love Actually is one of the most-watched Christmas films each year.

The film features 10 intertwining love stories, but there were originally additional romantic plotlines – some were cut in the final editing process.

Remember the infamous scene in *A Christmas Story* when Flick's tongue is frozen to a pole – and he is eventually rescued by firemen?

In shooting, the startling illusion was created with the aid of a hidden suction device.

It took the art department for *Elf* weeks to create the elaborate store set for the fight between Buddy and Santa. Because the actors had to smash the set, they had to get the scene right in one take.

What would Charles Dickens have made of the wise-cracking, all-singing, all-dancing puppets in *The Muppet Christmas Carol*? In his role as Ebenezer Scrooge, Michael Caine vowed to act "like I'm working with the Royal Shakespeare Company".

His tactic seems to have worked. For many, this version is the best adaptation of Dickens's classic tale.

The parade scenes from the 1947 movie *Miracle on 34th Street* had to be shot in a single day.

Rather than use special effects, the movie's producers decided to shoot the scenes during the actual 1946 Thanksgiving Day Parade in New York – putting some time constraints on the filming schedule.

66

I believe, I believe, it's silly, but I believe.

99

Miracle on 34th Street, *1947*

Highest-Grossing

CHRISTMAS FILMS

1. *The Grinch* (2018)

2. *Home Alone* (1990)

3. *Dr Seuss' How The Grinch Stole Christmas* (2000)

4. *A Christmas Carol* (2009)

5. *The Polar Express* (2004)

6. *Elf* (2003)

7. *The Holiday* (2006)

8. *The Santa Clause* (1994)

9. *Daddy's Home 2* (2017)

10. *The Nutcracker and the Four Realms* (2018)

"

Just because you
can't see something,
doesn't mean
it doesn't exist.

"

The Santa Clause, *1994*

66

Seeing is believing, but sometimes the most real things in the world are the things we can't see.

99

Chris Van Allsburg, The Polar Express, *1985*

"

I suppose it all started with the snow. You see, it was a very special kind of snow. A snow that made the happy happier, and the giddy even giddier.

"

Frosty the Snowman, 1969

CHAPTER SIX

CHRISTMAS CAROLS AND SONGS

Christmas music – whether a traditional carol like "Hark the Herald Angels Sing" or a jingly tune like "Rockin' Around the Christmas Tree" – is as much a part of the festive season as Christmas trees, Santa and mince pies. Read on to discover fascinating facts about your favourite festive songs.

In medieval times, "carol" meant a round-dance with song.

The word comes from the old French *carole*, which derived from the Latin *choraula* and the Greek word *choros*.

Carols used to be sung during all four seasons, but only the tradition of singing them at Christmas has survived.

One of the first carols to be sung was "Angel's Hymn", written in 129 CE.

From around this time, Christian-themed songs grew in popularity as the pagan songs celebrating the winter solstice, Saturnalia, began to die away.

The "Boar's Head Carol" is one of the oldest printed carols, dating from 1521. It describes the ancient custom of sacrificing a boar to be consumed at a Yuletide feast.

The boar's head, with an apple in its mouth, was carried into a banquet hall on a gold or silver dish as trumpets sounded and minstrels sang.

One of the darkest of all Christmas carols is the 16th-century lament "Coventry Carol".

Describing an event in the Book of Matthew known as the "Slaughter of the Innocents" – when King Herod ordered the killing of all male children under the age of two – the carol is written from the perspective of mothers soothing their doomed baby boys.

One of the most popular carols, "Away in a Manger", was written by an American in the 1880s.

The anonymous writer claimed it was the work of the German reformer Martin Luther, so that for decades it was known as "Luther's Cradle Song".

The words to "Come All You Faithful"
have been attributed to Francis Wade,
a Jacobite who supported the exiled
Stuart royal family. Some experts
believe there is a subversive message
hidden in the lyrics rallying support
for Bonnie Prince Charlie.

As "Bethlehem" was a Jacobite code
word for "England", they claim
"Joyful and Triumphant, O Come Ye,
O Come Ye to Bethlehem"
really means, "Joyful and Triumphant
Jacobites, Come to England."

The much-loved carol "Silent Night" set the scene for a truce during the First World War. On Christmas Eve in 1914, British troops heard soldiers singing *"Stille Nacht"*.

They responded by singing the carol in English. Eventually, the troops emerged from the trenches to meet each other in No Man's Land, exchange gifts and even play football together.

Fighting resumed the following day.

The first Christmas song to mention Santa Claus was Benjamin Hanby's "Up On The Housetop".

Written in 1864, it drew inspiration from Clement Moore's poem **"Twas the Night Before Christmas"**.

THE 12 DAYS OF CHRISTMAS

The origins of the song "The 12 Days of Christmas" are a little murky. Most historians believe it was intended to be a "memory and forfeits" game, in which singers tested their recall of all the gifts. If they made a mistake, they would have to award their opponent a "forfeit", such as a kiss or a favour of some kind.

The cumulative gifts given to the young lady by her eager suitor in "The 12 Days of Christmas" add up to 364 – one for each day of a traditional year minus Christmas Day.

The answer is NOT 78!

JINGLE BELLS

is the number-one Christmas song of all time – even though it makes no mention of Christmas!

It was written by an American, James Lord Pierpont, in 1857, under the name "The One-Horse Open Sleigh". The jingling bells were not festive adornments, but a legal requirement – fines were issued to sleigh racers who didn't "jingle all the way"!

The 1958 hit
"The Chipmunk Song
(Christmas Don't
Be Late)" topped the
Billboard Hot 100 Pop
Singles chart that year.

It was the first
Christmas tune to ever
do so.

With 50 million copies sold, Bing Crosby's "White Christmas" is the best-selling Christmas song of all time.

It was written by Irving Berlin – who was Jewish and did not celebrate Christmas – for the movie *Holiday Inn*.

"

Unless we make
Christmas an occasion
to share our blessings,
all the snow in Alaska
won't make it 'white'.

"

Bing Crosby

CHRISTMAS CHARTS

The Top 10 most streamed festive hits

1. "All I Want for Christmas" – Mariah Carey

2. "Last Christmas" – Wham!

3. "Fairytale of New York" – The Pogues with Kirsty MacColl

4. "Merry Christmas Everyone" – Shakin' Stevens

5. "Do They Know It's Christmas"
– Band Aid

6. "It's Beginning to Look a Lot Like
Christmas"
– Michael Buble

7. "Step Into Christmas" – Elton John

8. "Santa Tell Me" – Ariana Grande

9. "I Wish it Could Be Christmas
Everyday" – Wizzard

10. "Rockin' Around the Christmas Tree"
– Brenda Lee

"The Christmas Song",
more often referred to as
"Chestnuts Roasting on an
Open Fire", was written during
a sweltering heatwave in the
summer of 1944.

The songwriters, Mel Tormé
and Bob Wells, began
writing the lyrics as a way of
distracting themselves from
the heat.

The original version of
"I Saw Mommy Kissing Santa
Claus" was recorded by 13-year-
old Jimmy Boyd in 1952. Several
radio stations banned it after the
Catholic Church claimed
the song promoted adultery.

After Jimmy met Church leaders
to explain that Santa was the
child's father (and the mother's
husband), the ban was lifted.

Shane MacGowan and Kirsty MacColl's parts for The Pogues' Christmas hit, "Fairytale of New York", were recorded separately – the pair never sang the song together in the studio.

The original lyrics to "Have Yourself a Merry Little Christmas" weren't very merry at all, with the words continuing, "It may be your last / Next year we may all be living in the past."

The song was jollied up for Judy Garland to sing in the film *Meet Me in St Louis*.

When Brenda Lee recorded "Rockin' Around the Christmas Tree" in 1958, she was only 13 years old.

"Last Christmas" by Wham!
is one of the best-loved
Christmas songs of all time.

However, George Michael was
sued by singer Barry Manilow,
who claimed the Christmas
hit was too similar to his song
"Can't Smile Without You".

The case was eventually
settled out of court.

"

Have yourself a merry
little Christmas,

Let your heart be light,

From now on,

Our troubles will be out
of sight.

"

Hugh Martin and Ralph Blane,
"Have Yourself a Merry Little Christmas"